BCS

Improving Productivity Using IT

Level 3

Using Microsoft® Office

D1340174

Release BCS013v2

Published by:

CiA Training Ltd
Business & Innovation Centre
Sunderland Enterprise Park
Sunderland
SR5 2TA
United Kingdom

Tel: +44 (0) 191 549 5002
Fax: +44 (0) 191 549 9005

E-mail: info@ciatraining.co.uk
Web: www.ciatraining.co.uk

ISBN: 978-1-86005-828-8

First published 2010

Aims

To provide the knowledge and techniques necessary to plan, evaluate and improve procedures involving the use of complex and non-routine IT tools and systems which will improve the productivity of work activities.

Objectives

After completing the guide the user will be able to:

- Select IT tools and techniques to complete a given task

- Undertake research that enables you to understand what expectations and requirements must be met by the task solution

- Understand what is required by a task and the best way to achieve it

- Evaluate the outcome of the task including strengths and weaknesses

- Identify improvements relevant to future work

- Offer support and advice to other users

Notes

The BCS assessment for this unit is divided into two parts – **Performance** and **Knowledge**. In the **Performance** part of the test the user will carry out tasks based on a scenario using an application of their choice. This guide has been designed to reinforce the skills needed to choose the most appropriate software for the task, and then to justify that choice in the **Knowledge** part of the test.

It is assumed that the user is competent in the use of their chosen application(s) to a level 3 standard. Training in any specific software application is outside the scope of this guide, and is provided in accompanying CiA Training titles.

Contents

Section 1
Plan and Select

By the end of this Section you should be able to:

Explain the Purpose for using IT

Analyse what methods, skills and resources will be needed

Plan how to carry out tasks using IT

Analyse any factors that may affect the task

Select IT systems and software applications

Explain why particular IT applications were chosen

Explain any legal or local guidelines or constraints

Exercise 1 - Purpose

Guidelines

An advanced IT user can plan and review their use of IT tools, most of which will be complex and non-routine. They will then be able to devise solutions which improve productivity and help to streamline business processes. They will be able to work on their own to produce a solution and will also be able to offer support and advice to other IT users.

The solution to any problem starts with the problem itself. The first step in developing an IT solution must be the correct identification of what exactly is required. Questions to be asked are:

- What is the purpose of the IT task?

- Who will be using it?

- What information and explanation will be required?

- How and where will it be used? For example, on screen or as a printed document?

- When is the solution required? How long do you have to finish it?

In a practical situation these questions will require you to communicate with the people involved. Hold meetings with those involved, both collectively and individually. Gather information on the problems facing them and investigate their requirements for a solution. Make sure you know what the problem actually is; people may be talking about the symptoms of the problem rather than its cause.

The intended audience can have a major impact on both the content and style of the final document, e.g. a report on company performance may be different if intended for the general staff or for the Financial Director, and a letter to a friend would look different to a business letter to a customer.

With technical content you should also be aware of the level of knowledge the audience has of the subject and plan the document accordingly. Too much explanation of areas with which the audience is familiar may cause them to lose interest. Likewise, too little explanation for an audience with little or no subject knowledge may have the same effect.

Consider too the cultural background of the audience and make sure that both the content and style are relevant and appropriate.

In the assessment for this unit, you will be given a scenario in which the purpose of the task is well defined. You should read the details of the scenario carefully and make sure you can answer all the questions listed above.

continued over

Exercise 1 - Continued

Having specific and documented aims is useful as it helps keep the development 'on course'. Constantly checking against the original project aims can prevent effort being spent on areas that are not relevant.

Examples

Four sample scenarios will be used throughout this guide to illustrate the points of each exercise. Each will represent one of the software applications that could be used – at present – in the assessment (word processing using *Word*, spreadsheets using *Excel*, presentations using *PowerPoint*, and databases using *Access*).

Sample Scenarios:

A. You are asked to produce a status report on a currently active project. All of the necessary content exists as documents, text files, spreadsheets, etc. It all needs to be collected in one file, and formatted professionally with headers and footers, sections, consistent styles, captions, contents and index.

The final file could be annotated and sent out for review.

B. You are provided with an old presentation introducing a college to prospective students and asked to bring it up to date with sounds, animation and links to appropriate external data. It is required that different pages of the information will be made available depending on the courses that the prospective students are considering. Instruction for the process should to be provided. It should be ready for viewing in one hour.

C. You are provided with sets of figures relating to the performance of a small manufacturing company, including production by product and month, and sales by product and area. You are asked to provide various analyses of these figures, including charts and tables where appropriate, to help the company plan next year's strategy.

D. You are asked to improve the local beauty salon's diary system. All data is currently stored in three separate spreadsheets; one containing customer contact details, one containing staff details, and one containing appointments. You will need to improve the current system and make it easier for others to find, manage and update information. In particular, the new system should produce a report on-screen showing upcoming appointments for the next 24 hours. It should be ready for use in one hour.

i	*It should be stressed that these are CiA Training sample scenarios, meant only to illustrate some of the features of the assessment. They have no connection with any scenario which may form part of the testing of this unit.*

Exercise 2 - Application Choice

Guidelines

With the purposes of the task established, it is now time to consider possible IT solutions. In a practical situation it is worth investigating whether an IT solution is appropriate at all, or whether a combination of applications may be required. In the assessment for this unit it is assumed that a single software application will be appropriate.

You will have to decide and justify which software application is best suited to your given task. The following notes will help you to understand the differences between the common software applications and appreciate their separate uses.

At this level, you have to be able to critically compare the alternative methods available from different applications and decide which one is best to produce the intended outcome.

Word processing

One of the most widely used applications on computers are word processing programs. Word processing software such as *Microsoft Word* enables you to produce professional looking, well-styled documents for many different purposes. Typical word processing solutions include:

- Letters/Mail shots

- Brochures/newsletters

- Reports

Word processing is appropriate for any task that requires a largely text based solution, particularly if printed output is required. Entry, presentation and formatting of text are easily handled by an application such as *Microsoft Word*. It is also easy to include different types of objects such as images, tables and charts. This can also be done with an application like *Microsoft Publisher*, but many more specialised features are available in *Word*, such as automatic creation of referencing like contents and index pages, and the ability to merge documents with data in tabular form to produce mail shots, etc.

One advantage of word processing applications for solutions that will be used by other people is their widespread use and acceptance. More people will be familiar with word processing than probably any other application.

Presentation

A presentation is an appropriate application for any task that requires a more visual result with text restricted to brief notes or bullet points, particularly if on-screen viewing is required. *Microsoft PowerPoint* allows complex and impressive presentations to be produced with relative ease.

continued over

Exercise 2 - Continued

The presentations can be used as on-screen shows controlled by a presenter, overhead projector shows, or for creating automatically run presentations for use as promotions in public places, or display on a network such as the Internet. They can include text in any format, pictures, organisation charts, graphs, sound and film clips, and information from the Internet. A slide show can incorporate text animation and slide effects.

As well as slides, *PowerPoint* can produce presentation notes, handouts, printouts of slides and outlines of text. Presentations are excellent tools for promotional or staff training purposes.

Spreadsheet

Spreadsheets are most commonly used to manipulate figures. They can be used in:

- Accounting

- Cash flows

- Budgets, forecasts, etc.

- Transaction analysis

Any task involving the use of numbers can be done using a spreadsheet. A spreadsheet package such as *Microsoft Excel* can help in the processing of tabular information (usually numbers). The spreadsheet stores information in rows (across the screen) and columns (down the screen), forming a worksheet (the *Excel* term for one single spreadsheet).

The biggest advantage that a spreadsheet has over other methods of manipulating data – using a table in a word processing application for example – is its ability to constantly update figures without the need to redo any calculations. Once a spreadsheet is set up correctly, with formulas and functions, any changes in data are recalculated automatically and accurately.

Spreadsheets can also take basic data and present it in an attractive way, using formatted lists, tables or graphs. More complex features are available such as conditional formatting, data validation, complex formulas, linked data, hyperlinks, and a range of chart types. One particular advantage in using a spreadsheet application is its ability to handle complex analysis tasks, using for example, pivot tables, data tables, scenarios, sorting/filtering and sub-totalling.

Databases

Databases are efficient at handling large amounts of data held in a number of different locations. *Microsoft Access* is an application which allows databases to be built and managed without knowledge of programming languages.

continued over

Exercise 2 - Continued

Data in a database is held in tables and if there is a logical connection between the data, the tables can be linked together (related). When used properly this should mean that no item of data is ever held in more than one place.

Objects can be built in *Access* to make it easier to find, manage and update data, such as:

- Queries. These allow specific data to be extracted from linked tables using a range of criteria.

- Forms. These allow data to be viewed and/or updated using specifically formatted screens.

- Reports. These allow data to be extracted, analysed and presented, using specifically formatted layouts.

Examples

A.   The report scenario requires a word processing solution. This is because the solution involves extensive use of text, and the application of complex formatting and cross referencing functions. If the solution required the newsletter to be viewed on screen (on an intranet for example) then a a presentation or web site solution could be considered, but given the focus on text, word processing should be the selected method.

  The solution could also have used an application such as *Microsoft Publisher*, but at this level, word processing would probably be chosen because of greater familiarity and better choice of referencing functions.

B.   The student introduction scenario requires a presentation solution. This is because the scenario requires easy links to movies and sounds and interaction from the user. A presentation application such as *PowerPoint* is the ideal way to achieve this.

C.   The planning scenario requires a spreadsheet solution. This is indicated because the solution will mainly involve the processing and presentation of numeric information. The solution could also have been created using a database application such as *Microsoft Access*, but at this level, a spreadsheet would be the simplest alternative and offers a greater range of analysis tools.

D.   The beauty salon diary scenario would be best handled with a database solution. This is because the existing data is held in a number of different locations and it would be more efficient to have them related in a single system. Also, the process of finding, managing and updating data can be made much easier by using database features such as Forms, Queries and Reports.

Exercise 3 - Justification

Guidelines

Having compared IT applications and decided on one which meets the needs of the current task, you should be prepared to justify your choice of application. This includes justifying the use of an IT solution rather than a manual approach. Although for the purposes of this qualification it is assumed that an IT solution will be implemented, you should be aware that in the real world the overall use of IT within an organisation would have to be considered before coming to any conclusions about solutions.

Within an organisation, there may be a variety of issues which affect people's attitude to IT.

- People who have never had exposure to IT systems can be wary of it because of unfamiliarity.

- People may distrust IT because they see it as intrusive and capable of monitoring their activity.

- People may favour IT solutions because they like the flexibility and the possibility of home working, for example.

- Some see IT systems as environmentally friendly because they can reduce the use of paper. Alternatively, others consider them environmentally unfriendly because of their reliance on electricity.

In general, however, there are many benefits which can result from using an IT solution:

- For any given task it will usually be quicker to use an IT solution. Usually an IT system will produce results (e.g. calculations, documents) more quickly than a manual process. This is particularly true for repeated tasks, as there is always the 'overhead time' of producing the original solution which will not apply when the task is repeated.

- An IT solution should be more convenient to produce as all the necessary information and functions will be available from a single point – the computer.

- An IT solution should produce more consistently high quality results, without the time and expense of employing specialists.

- An IT solution should produce more consistently accurate results. This of course depends on the input data being accurate, enabling the business to manage information efficiently.

- An IT solution should have a productivity benefit, as staff will spend less time performing and checking manual tasks.

continued over

Exercise 3 - Continued

- An IT solution should have a cost benefit to the organisation (should all the points listed above be true).

- An IT solution should help to produce more integrated and consistent (streamlined) processes throughout an organisation. This can result from using the same fonts, colour schemes, imagery, etc., across solutions, and by integration and reuse of data. For example, the results in a spreadsheet can be easily used later in the creation of a report.

It should also be noted that there are potential negative aspects to IT solutions:

- An IT solution has a development time and cost. This should be weighed up against the time and cost benefits.

- Be aware that people who will be asked to run any new IT system must have the necessary skills to do the tasks efficiently. This may involve retraining.

Examples

A. Word processing is the ideal solution for the report task. It is a quick and simple way to produce a good looking document with all the required structure. The only alternative would be to use specialist printers and publishers which would involve much more time and money. Non IT staff could easily take over the production of future editions if a template were produced.

B. Similarly, an application such as *PowerPoint* is the only practical way that a professional looking presentation could be produced easily and quickly. Alternatives would be to employ specialist film makers.

C. The purpose of the planning task is to analyse a range of numeric data and present the results in a professional manner. Using a spreadsheet application to do this will create an efficient solution with the minimum of manual processes. Once the original data is entered, all the analysis can be produced with guaranteed accuracy.

D. Using a database for the salon diary will integrate the data from the different spreadsheets into a single system. By creating forms and reports, the system can be easily managed by personnel with little IT experience. Some of the required output for the task could be achieved by manipulating the original spreadsheets in *Excel*, but there would be no integration between them. Expertise in *Excel* would also be required for operation.

Exercise 4 - Planning

Guidelines

When the purpose of the task has been identified, the details of the project need to be planned.

When planning your chosen task, some thought should be given to how you are going to obtain the desired result. The planning should include the content and explain where that content fits into the finished resource. Think about who the resource is for, how they would like the information to be presented and how it is to be used; consider potential problems that may arise.

At this level your planning should pay particular attention to these points:

- The application to be used.

- Source material. What source information will be required and where will it come from? If it is an external source, some evaluation and validation may be necessary.

- Content. Consider the actual data that will be contained in the system and how it will be presented to users. Are there any special requirements for the format and structure of the system output? There may be a house style which must be adopted, or the use of specified corporate images and logos.

- Priorities. If there is more source material than is needed for the solution's content, what or who will decide the priorities for which information will be used? If there are time constraints, which features must be included and which could be left out?

- Resources. What resources will be necessary to run the solution? For example, is any extra hardware or software needed, and will any extra personnel be required? Resources can include such things as:

  o Hardware - how many personal computers are available and what specification are they? Are they powerful enough?

  o Software - what software applications are available? Can they open and use a solution created in a particular application?

  o People - how many people are available to operate any new system and will any more be required?

  o The skills and capabilities of the potential users - keep things simple and do not create a solution that will be technically beyond the users' abilities to operate. Be aware of what skills will be required, and consider a training process if necessary.

continued over

Exercise 4 - Continued

o   Your skills and capabilities - do not attempt a project that will be technically beyond your ability to develop successfully.

o   Support - what level and amount of support will be available, for both you and the end-user?

o   The needs of the organisation - you should not be developing projects for the sake of it. There should be clear definable objectives from the point of view of the organisation which justify the project. These objectives can be reviewed on completion to see how well they have been met.

Examples

A.   In the report scenario, all content would be provided, but there may be more than is required. Select the most appropriate data based on the task specification. The report is to present status information on a specific project; any information not relevant to this purpose should be omitted. However, part of the specification was that the final report should be professionally presented, so pay particular attention to layout by breaking the content into logical sections.

B.   In the introduction presentation scenario, all content would be provided, but again there may be more than is needed to meet the requirements of the solution. Select the most appropriate data based on the task specification. Include content that will be relevant to new students. This may include basic information about the college, map of the main campus, details of the individual courses on offer, etc.

C.   The planning spreadsheet would probably have less emphasis on style and layout, although of course it should be clear and easy to understand. The main requirements of the system will be that it is accurate and easy to operate. All starting data would be provided, but check to see if it is all required. For example, any details of individual transactions would probably not be required; it would be sufficient to show only summarised information.

D.   For the diary database system, it will be necessary to define what input and output is required of the system, and design the database appropriately. As the data already exists on spreadsheets it is possible to use this data to create database tables which are then maintained in *Access*, or to link the database tables to the spreadsheets, in which case the data would still be maintained in *Excel*.

Exercise 5 - Factors

Guidelines

In completing any task there are a great number of factors to be taken into account to ensure a successful solution. Many of them have been covered in previous exercises but they can be summarised here with some additional detail.

- Resources - are all of the required resources going to be available?

- Information - is all of the information required by the task going to be available?

- Timescale - are there limits as to when the solution must be available?

- Costs - are there limits as to the development costs of the solution?

- Style and format - are there any particular requirements for style (eye-catching, simple, amusing, etc.) which may affect the form of the solution?

- External factors - what impact will the solution have on people outside the organisation, e.g. Customers, Suppliers, Public?

- Personal preference - are there any strongly held personal preferences which may affect the form of the solution? The importance of this factor depends largely on the importance of the person with the preferences.

- Advance steps - are there any steps, maybe arising from the points above, which will require completing in advance of the task? For example, ordering new hardware/software, or evaluating data sources.

Examples

- ❖ For any scenario used in this assessment, the factors that may affect the task will be included in the scenario specification. For example, restrictions on time, cost or appearance. When planning the solution, take all such factors into account.

Exercise 6 - Local Constraints

Guidelines

As well as the requirements and constraints of the individual task which have been discussed previously, there may be more general constraints. Some of these may be in the form of security considerations or local constraints such as existing 'house styles' in force within the organisation.

- House styles. In your chosen task you may already be required to format all work to specified house styles. These are formatting parameters that are set by an organisation to be applied to all documents used. They will include features such as which text fonts and sizes should be used in any given part of a document and which colour schemes and logos should be included. There may be variations of house style for different applications, e.g. for internal and external documents and for particular projects or product brands within the organisation.

- Security. Any solution should take into account data security. Data security can be broadly divided into two areas: security against data loss and security against unauthorised access. The effects of data loss can be minimised by ensuring that your solution is backed up, i.e. copied to an alternative location, preferably off-site, and that it is included in any existing regular backup procedures.

- Protection against unauthorised access will depend on how sensitive the information is in your solution. **Information security** is a term used to describe methods for ensuring that data stored on a computer system is protected against being compromised, or against unauthorised access. It can include such features as:

    o   A user ID/password policy to cover access to all computers

    o   Separate user-level security on individual systems/data files

    o   Designated personnel responsible for each level of security

    o   Antivirus measures, including use of a firewall

    o   Procedures for educating staff about their responsibilities regarding information security

    o   Security is particularly important when the data contains personal data about individuals. Storage and use of such data is governed by strict legal regulations, contravention of which can lead to criminal proceedings. All users of such systems must be aware of the relevant legislation, i.e. the Data Protection Act. This is covered in the next exercise

continued over

Exercise 6 - Continued

Examples

A.   The report task will almost certainly involve the use of 'house styles' to ensure that the publication is representative of the organisation's image. Any style requirements will be given with the original specification.

There is probably no requirement for security on such a system, although the content could be password protected to avoid mischievous alterations.

B.   An introduction presentation will probably also involve the same house styles considerations as the report task. Although all required images sounds and movies will be supplied, in a real situation they should all be checked for copyright issues.

C.   A spreadsheet solution to calculate pay is less likely to have house style and copyright issues, but will certainly have security and data protection implications.

D.   Database objects such as forms and reports can be formatted, so they may require application of 'house styles' or company logos. Security involving user IDs and passwords may be an issue if the system can be accessed from a public area, and if the system becomes an important feature of the business, regular and comprehensive backups will be vital.

Exercise 7 - Legal Constraints

Guidelines

IT and electronic communication now form an important part of many peoples' lives, so it is not surprising that a large amount of regulation and legislation exists to control it. Many of these could be constraints could affect your solution, and some major examples are listed here.

- **Copyright**. Any image, text file or other item in print or on the Internet is considered to be the copyright of the person or organisation that created it. So unless you have explicit permission, you cannot use or distribute any material obtained from the World Wide Web.

- **User Licence**. Normally when you buy any piece of software, you purchase a licence to use the software in a single location, so giving away copies for others to use is illegal. Organisations will often purchase multiple user licences, which allows them to run a certain number of copies (but no more) within their organisation.

- **Data Protection Act**. An organisation which stores any personal data referring to any identifiable individuals is bound by the current version of this Act. In summary, this requires that all such data shall be:

  - Obtained and processed fairly and lawfully

  - Processed only for one or more specified and lawful purposes

  - Adequate, relevant and not excessive for those purposes

  - Accurate and kept up to date

  - Kept for the original purpose only and for no longer than is necessary.

  - Processed in line with the rights of the individual

  - Secure and protected against loss, damage and inappropriate processing

  - Not transferred to other countries unless they also have data protection

- **Computer Misuse Act**. This act covers the unauthorised access by individuals into computer systems, sometimes known as computer 'hacking'.

- **Consumer Rights**. In principle, buying goods or services electronically online is covered by the same consumer rights as buying from a shop, with some extra entitlements such as an order confirmation and a 'cooling off' period.

continued over

Exercise 7 - Continued

- **Health and Safety**. The Health and Safety at Work legislation (HASAW) has many regulations referring to computer installations, such as suitability and accessibility of equipment (keyboards, screens, mouse mats, etc.), and time spent using equipment.

- **Accessibility**. Computer installations should, wherever possible, be accessible to anyone regardless of their age, gender, origin or physical disability.

- **Inappropriate Content**. The displayed content of any computer system is governed by the same laws relating to offensive or obscene content as for printed material. In addition, individual organisations may have their own guidelines on this subject.

Examples

A. Copyright laws and regulations on inappropriate content would apply to the project report solution. If the new project is particularly sensitive then security of the data may be a consideration.

B. The presentation example will have the same considerations as the report.

C. If the performance review system holds any details referring to individuals, the security and legal constraints are likely to be much more significant.

D. The database example will have the same considerations as the *Excel* system above.

    If any solution involved installing new computers or software applications, then Health and Safety and User Licence rules may be relevant. Access to the system should be limited to specific individuals (or departments), data files should be protected, and the person responsible for data protection should be made aware of the information that is being held within the system.

Exercise 8 - Revision

You are employed by a company specialising in 3 products and are given a task to calculate the optimal quantities to produce of each item in order to minimise costs and maximise profit. You must provide more than one option and produce a report which details the options. The task is to be completed in a *Microsoft Office* environment. You decide to use the **scenarios** feature of *Microsoft Excel* for the task.

1. Which of the following skills will be <u>necessary</u> for you to complete this task?

   a) Database skills

   b) Word processing skills

   c) Spreadsheet skills

   d) SQL skills

2. In the above scenario, which of the following resources will be <u>necessary</u> for you to complete this task?

   a) Printer

   b) Copy of *Microsoft Excel*

   c) Copy of *Microsoft PowerPoint*

   d) Scanner

3. In the above scenario, the following are all reasons for choosing an IT solution based on *Excel*. Which do you think is the <u>most</u> important in <u>this particular</u> example?

   a) Data can be presented in an attractive way

   b) Data can be manipulated and analysed

   c) Figures can be updated without you having to do any calculations

4. If you were given a bank of images copied from the Internet to include in a company brochure, which would be your main legal consideration?

   a) Software licensing

   b) Data Protection

   c) Copyright

i   *Answers are shown in the **Answers** section at the end of this guide.*

Section 2
Create Solution

By the end of this Section you should be able to:

Use IT systems and software to complete planned tasks and produce effective outcomes

Use shortcut techniques to improve overall efficiency

Exercise 9 - Create a Solution

Guidelines

When all planning is complete, the actual solution can be created using the selected application. Whilst developing the solutions, always remain aware of the relevant points of the scenario specification and of the constraints and factors that may arise from them. Make sure the solution takes them all into account.

It is not the purpose of this unit to test knowledge of the individual applications. The technical level required should be no more than that covered by the appropriate specific units at this level, e.g. word processing, spreadsheets. Solutions at this level will involve activities which are "complex and non-routine". To quote from the Assessment Specification for this unit, "[Users] will take considerable responsibility and autonomy, and be prepared to offer support and advice to others".

Any solution may be expected to involve basic IT techniques such as:

- Manipulation of files and folders

- Data entry and editing

- Transferring data between applications

- Presenting all output to a professional standard

Examples

A. Producing a report using *Word* could involve the following skills:

  o Formatting (fonts and backgrounds)

  o Creating and applying styles

  o Using sections

  o Embedding and linking objects from other applications

  o Using referencing functions such as Table of Contents and Indexing

  o Setting security options

  o Using tables.

continued over

Exercise 9 - Continued

This picture shows an example page of a suitable report.

continued over

Exercise 9 - Continued

This picture shows an example page of a suitable report.

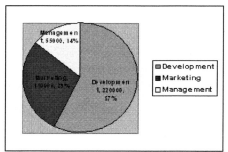

LaserMow   Project Report

1. Status Summary

1.1.   *Current Position*

The LaserMow project is on schedule in most areas of development. The prototype has completed preliminary tests with only minor updates being necessary. The marketing plan is also still on track for a launch of March next year.

The only area of concern is the issue of safety. Some safety agencies[1] are still reluctant to give full acceptance to the product without a much more stringent approach to perceived potential hazards. It seems that our reassurance "It'll be all right" is not proving acceptable. This situation is currently under review but will probably involve some additional technical input and subsequent slight delay.

1.2.   *Cost Estimates*

1.2.1. Overall

We have had to employ extra resource in the testing process because of the safety issues mentioned above. Present estimate is that this will add an extra £ 20,000 to the overall development budget.

1.2.2. Breakdown

The breakdown of costs by department is still roughly in line with original predictions.

Figure 1, Cost Breakdown

[1] Particularly the Animal Welfare agencies.

2   Project Department   17/06/2009

continued over

Exercise 9 - Continued

B.   Producing an introduction presentation using *PowerPoint* could involve the following skills:

- o   Slide formatting (fonts and backgrounds)

- o   Including objects from other applications

- o   Creation of customised slide shows

- o   Using charts

- o   Linking to external objects and web sites

The picture below shows two sample slides from a suitable presentation as an example

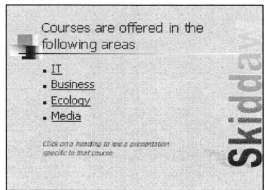

continued over

Exercise 9 - Continued

C.   Producing a performance review spreadsheet using *Excel* could involve the following skills:

   o   Conditional formatting

   o   Embedding and linking objects from other application

   o   Scenarios

   o   Pivot tables

   o   Charts

The picture below shows some sheets from a sample spreadsheet that could be used as a solution.

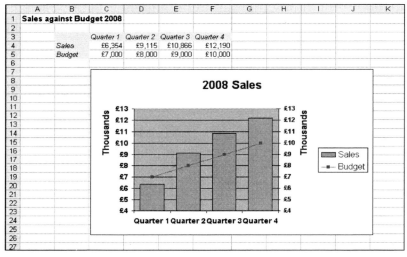

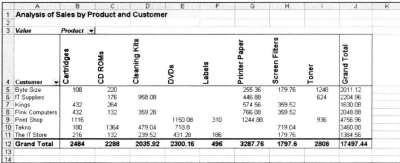

continued over

Exercise 9 - Continued

D.   Producing a booking and diary system using *Access* could involve the following skills:

- o   Importing data

- o   Creating relationships between tables

- o   Creating Queries

- o   Creating Forms

- o   Creating Reports

The picture below shows the relationship diagram and an example of a diary report from a sample database that could be used as a solution.

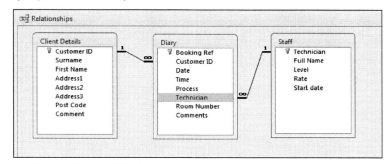

Exercise 10 - Improve Productivity

Guidelines

There are many simple techniques for improving your productivity when developing software solutions. Some of these techniques include:

Templates

A template is a framework for a standard document (including spreadsheets, presentations and databases) which can be saved and used as the basis for future documents. This can increase efficiency as the same layout does not have to be entered every time a new document is produced.

Templates are normal documents that are saved in a special **Templates** folder (often with a different file extension). When you create a new document, you can choose to base it on a template, saving you from starting from scratch. Templates are particularly useful for standard documents that are used frequently, such as letters to customers or frequently produced publications.

If you are creating a common solution to a problem, you may even find that ready-made templates are already available in the application you are using, or available for download via the Internet.

Macros

A **macro** records keystrokes and menu selections and then plays them back exactly as they were recorded. A macro can be created so that a commonly used sequence of steps can be saved once and repeated automatically many times afterwards (e.g. repeating changes to page settings, or entering a word, phrase or paragraph). The use of macros results in the more efficient production of documents. Once macros have been created, they can be used at any time in any document that uses the same template.

Shortcuts

There are various shortcuts that can be applied to IT solutions to make them more efficient. For example, program interfaces (e.g. toolbars) can be customised to include shortcuts to macros that have been created, or shortcuts to files or applications can be displayed on your **Desktop** or **Taskbar**.

Shared Files

Collaborating on documents with others is an efficient way to create new software solutions. It is possible to share most document types with others and track changes made to them. When they are returned to you, you can automatically compare those changes to your original document, review what changes have been made, and accept or reject them.

Exercise 11 - Revision

1. In which two of the following examples would the use of a template be the most appropriate?

    a) A letter to your bank

    b) A quarterly report showing sales for each department in a company

    c) A twice yearly mail shot promoting new products to customers on a database

    d) A report produced as part of a one off bid for a contract

2. Which of the following processes could best be replaced by a macro?

    a) Format each real name in a document as **Bold**

    b) Resize each image in a document as 10cm by 6cm with a dark blue border

    c) Crop each image in a document to highlight the relevant parts

3. Why is it appropriate to place a macro on a toolbar?

    a) Because it looks good

    b) Because it will not work otherwise

    c) Because it is more convenient to run

4. Why is it good practice to use styles in a template?

    a) They save time spent formatting

    b) All documents will have a consistent look

    c) They can help to create a corporate image

Section 3
Review and Adapt

By the end of this Section you should be able to:

Review ongoing use of IT tools and techniques

Evaluate whether selected IT tools were appropriate

Analyse the strengths and weaknesses of the solution

Describe ways to make further improvements

Review solutions

Exercise 12 - Review Techniques

Guidelines

When the solution has been completed, there should be a review of the effectiveness of the choices made. Information should be collected from a study of how the solution is operating.

There are many factors which can be considered when deciding whether the choice of tools and techniques were appropriate:

- Time - has the time taken to develop the solution been in line with the original plan? Would it have been quicker to use any alternative methods?

- Cost - similarly, has the cost of the development been as expected?

- Convenience - has the choice of IT tools for the task resulted in a more convenient, easy-to-use solution? Would it have been easier to use any alternative methods?

- Quality/accuracy - do the chosen IT tools provide sufficient quality and accuracy in the solution?

- Versatility - has the choice of IT tools for the task resulted in a versatile solution? Could it be easily adapted to other, related tasks? Could the information in the solution be easily presented in a different format, to be transferred to another application? Compare with other IT tools and techniques - has the choice of tools and approach been optimised? Does the solution offer a range of functions and facilities?

- Information access - are there any issues in accessing the necessary information for the solution? For example, does it require a network connection and/or a security password, or does it involve downloading data from the Internet? Downloading large amounts of data from the Internet can be a problem, particularly if only a slow speed Internet connection is available.

- Does the solution meet all legal requirements - have you considered issues such as copyright, the data protection act, etc. And is the solution accessible to everyone?

If any of the above factors indicated that the solution was not as efficient as it should be, you should be prepared to modify the approach as necessary.

Examples

- ❖ For all the solutions, information should be collected on how well the outcome matches the requirements and how easily the outcome was achieved. Pay particular attention to whether the tools and techniques turned out to be appropriate. For example, do you think using *Word* to produce the newsletter was the best choice of application? Could it have been done better or quicker using any other techniques?

Exercise 13 - Analyse

Guidelines

As part of the review of the IT solution it is useful to analyse the performance of the final system in terms of strengths and weaknesses.

Potential areas of strength could include:

- Clarity - does the format and layout of the final work make the presented information clear and easy to follow?

- Accuracy - is all information presented accurately?

- Reliability - can the solution be relied on to behave in a consistent manner and produce consistent information?

- Structure - is all information presented in a logical, structured manner?

- Quality - is the style and quality of the final work of a professional standard and does it create a good impression on the intended audience?

- Efficiency - is the solution efficient to use? Does it include time saving processes, etc?

- Convenience - is the solution is easy to use?

- Robustness - the solution should not fail, even under a range of conditions, and any exceptional conditions should be handled logically.

Potential areas of weakness would obviously include the reverse aspect of the features above:

- Muddled, unclear information.

- Inaccuracies in the presented information.

- Inconsistent behaviour and information.

- Unstructured information makes it difficult to locate required points.

- The style and quality of the final work is of a poor standard and creates a bad impression on the intended audience.

- Inefficient - a lot of extra time and effort are needed to use the solution.

- The solution is not easy to use.

- The system is prone to failing, locking, etc., with no adequate recovery procedures.

continued over

Exercise 13 - Continued

Examples

A.   In the report scenario, is all the included information relevant and presented in a clear and accurate way? Is there a template available and will it be relevant to future editions? Does the format make the information easy to read and understand?

B.   In the presentation scenario all of the above are relevant, but there may be other considerations. Is the solution easy for users to operate? Also, do the transitions, animations and links detract from the overall effectiveness?

C.   In the spreadsheet scenario has all input data been checked for accuracy? Has it been entered correctly? Are all formulas checked and accurate? Are the analysis displays easy to understand and do they present the information that is required?

D.   In the diary database, are all the tables linked correctly? Is all the required data available on all forms and reports? Are any automated effects, such as control buttons and macros, working correctly? Is the system easy to operate?

Exercise 14 - Review Outcomes

Guidelines

A detailed review of the actual output from the solution is an important feature of the task. The first reason for doing this is to check the solution with the aims and plans for the project to ensure that the original requirements have been met. The second reason is to correct any errors, omissions or unwanted side effects that may exist within the solution.

Steps that could be involved in this process include:

- Checking the solutions against the original requirements. This is where written evidence of the aims and objectives of the task would be very useful.

- Consulting with the intended audience/users of the solution to see if the solution meets their requirements and expectations.

- Producing sample outputs (drafts) from the system for analysis.

- Checking the quality of the source information.

- Spell check and proof read all output text. Note that spell checking will only identify unrecognised words. It will not generally find words used incorrectly, e.g. *horse* instead of *house*, or *her* instead of *here*, so manual proof reading is always recommended.

- If the solution depends on numerical calculations, make sure they are tested with dummy data and compare the results with the expected results obtained by manual calculation. Ideally the solution will be tested with a range of input data, including extreme values to check that they are handled correctly.

- Check all output for suitability so that it will not cause offence to any member of the target audience.

- Check all output for compliance with legal requirements such as copyright or data protection laws.

- Be aware of what effect any mistakes in your solution will have on others.

- Are other users able to produce a final result of the intended/required standard?

- Are there features that could be added to improve the efficiency of the users of the solution, or of the organisation as a whole?

continued over

Exercise 14 - Continued

Although much of this section is concerned with reviewing the outcomes and implications of your own choices, the situation may arise when you are required to analyse the selections and work of others.

You may be called on to apply the skills and techniques you have learnt from this course to assessing the outcomes of other peoples' efforts.

There are, however, extra factors to be considered when others are involved. It is important to review and present your findings professionally without involving subjective opinion or personal criticism. You should offer feedback in a positive manner, emphasising ways in which the work could be enhanced and improved rather than listing faults. Other than these considerations, the techniques described in this section for reviewing and analysing selections can be applied equally well to the work of others.

Examples

A. Check that the report meets the original requirements. Is it professionally structured and formatted? Is it free from spelling and grammar mistakes? Is the content presented clearly and logically? Make sure that it does not contain any offensive, inappropriate or copyright protected content.

B. Check that the presentation meets the original requirements. Are all links working completely as planned? Does it display relevant summary information in a professional way? Is it easy for users to operate? Check with users that it communicates the desired information. Make sure that it does not contain any offensive, inappropriate or copyright protected content.

C. Check that the spreadsheet meets the original requirements. Is all starting data correctly set up? Is all displayed data clear and unambiguous? Are users of the system happy that it supplies them with the information and analysis that they need?

D. Check that the diary system has met expectations. Is it easy to operate and is it an improvement over the previous system? Does the diary report provide the required level of information and control?

Exercise 15 - Improvements

Guidelines

After testing and reviewing the solution, it may become clear that there are a variety of ways in which the work could be improved.

- Correcting any mistakes. This will obviously improve the quality of the work.

- Responding to feedback. It may become obvious when the solution is actually operating that there is a better way for parts of the process to work. For example, these may make the overall process easier to use or less prone to errors.

- Give feedback to users on their strengths and weaknesses and on potential improvements that they could make.

- Learning new techniques. This may mean that some features of the project could be achieved in different ways, which would improve the operation of the solution.

- Adding automated IT features to the solution such as macros and shortcuts. This will improve the efficiency of the solution.

- In systems that require input of data, the data entry interfaces could be streamlined to increase efficiency.

- Minimising the impact that the new system has on other people's work. The effectiveness of a solution is reduced if it requires an increase in work in a different area.

Examples

- ❖ Any solution should be analysed with respect to the points listed above.

Exercise 16 - Revision

You are employed by a company specialising in 3 products and are given a task to calculate the optimal quantities to produce of each item in order to minimise costs and maximise profit. You must provide more than one option and produce a report which details the options. The task is to be completed in a *Microsoft Office* environment. You decide to use the **scenarios** feature of *Microsoft Excel* for the task.

1. Which of these statements best confirms that the chosen IT solution was appropriate for the task?

    a) "The report looks attractive."

    b) "We will need a better printer for this report."

    c) "Well done, we now know which product mix will result in the biggest profit."

    d) "Product 'c' is most popular."

2. From the following statements, pick one which represents a strength of the solution.

    a) Different product mixes can be analysed when we want

    b) The details in the database of products could be more complete

    c) Staff don't know how to manipulate the data

    d) The report is easily accessible on the network

3. Which two of the following would best represent an improvement to your solution?

    a) Apply a corporate logo to the report

    b) Produce a simple user instruction document

    c) Add an update process for the product database

    d) Restrict access to the report

Section 4
Develop and Test

By the end of this Section you should be able to:

Review the benefits and drawbacks of IT tools

Analyse ways to increase productivity and efficiency

Develop solutions to improve productivity

Test solutions to ensure they work as intended

Exercise 17 - Review Benefits

Guidelines

Using IT tools to develop solutions in a business environment will usually produce both benefits and drawbacks with respect to productivity. Some of these have been discussed in the course of this guide but they can be summarised here.

Benefits:

- Faster achievement of output
- Higher quality output
- More automated system – frees staff for other tasks
- Less need for outside specialists
- More consistent, reliable output
- Ability to integrate with other IT systems

Drawbacks:

- Cost of development
- Retraining costs
- Cost of extra resources, e.g. computers, software
- Dependence on technology

Examples

A. The main benefits of the report solution are that it produces a high quality outcome quickly which is much more readable than the original data, without the need for specialist staff.

B. The main benefits of the presentation solution are that it produces a high quality, flexible outcome which is easily accessible, without the need for specialist staff.

C. The main benefits of the spreadsheet solution are that it produces a reliable, useful analysis of a large amount of raw data, which then has the potential to streamline business operations by assisting informed decision making.

D. The main benefits of the database solution are that it integrates all data in a single system and makes it easy both to input data and extract any kind of analysis without the need for specialist staff.

Exercise 18 - Develop Solutions

Guidelines

When an IT solution is reviewed, it may become clear that changes could be made to improve it. Of course, any improvement in productivity would have to be balanced against the cost of developing the solution further. Some reasons to justify that cost include:

- Achieve the same result in less time

- Achieve the same result for less money

- Achieve greater output in the same time

- Achieve higher quality output

- Free staff for other tasks

One way to achieve these aims is to reduce the manual component of the task and allow the computer to handle more of it, i.e. to have more automated processes. For example, you could use conditional calculations to deal with different situations automatically without user intervention, e.g. calculate different discount rates depending on the total sales value for a record.

Furthermore, any features where data can be manipulated automatically rather than needing to be manually processed will make the solution quicker and easier to operate, less likely to produce errors, and therefore more efficient.

When data from external sources is required within a system, it is usually better to create a link to that data rather than copy it or re-enter it. Linking to external data means that whenever the source data is changed in any way, the most recent version of that data will always be used without any user intervention.

Other examples of automated features would be:

- Use a macro, so that one action by the user can run a series of processes in a fixed sequence

- Create shortcuts, so that commonly used features can be started quickly

- Customise menus and toolbars to include shortcuts and macros

- Create templates so that consistent results can be achieved more quickly if the task is required again

continued over

Exercise 18 - Continued

Examples

A. The productivity of the report task could be improved by creating a template for the solution before any content is added. Subsequent reports could then be produced merely by opening the template and adding new content.

B. If the introduction presentation is a one-off project, then there is not much scope for increasing productivity. Linking the slide content to other files would mean that updates could be made easily to the original objects using the relevant applications and these changes would be automatically reflected in the presentation. Defining a template with master slides would benefit the production of any future versions of the presentation.

C. A template of the analysis spreadsheet would make it easy to produce new spreadsheets for each week. Data validation and formula auditing could reduce the possibility of input and calculation errors and conditional formatting could highlight exceptional results.

D. Once all the required data is held within a database, a range of analysis and reporting processes are available. For instance, queries highlighting double-booking of staff or resources could be easily produced. The database could also be redeveloped into other systems which use the same data, such as analysis of client business or an automatic invoicing system.

Exercise 19 - Test Solution

Guidelines

The final version of the developed solution should always be tested by the designer and end users.

- As mentioned previously, it is important that the results of the task are compared to the original plan requirements.

- A final check can be made of spelling, calculations and content.

- Particularly check any automated features or improvements which have been added to the solution later in the process. Do any templates, macros and shortcuts work as intended?

Examples

A.   Check that the report meets the original requirements. Is it free from spelling and grammar mistakes? If there is a template for the finished solution, does it open and allow content to be easily added?

B.   Check that the presentation meets the original requirements. If there are links to any external material, do the links work correctly? If there is a template for the finished solution, does it open and allow content to be easily added?

C.   Check that the spreadsheet meets the original requirements. If there are any automated features, do they work as intended? If there are any added features such as data export of reports, do they work as intended?

D.   Check that the database meets the original requirements. If there are any automated features such as linked tables or control button macros, do they work as intended? If there are any added features such as queries and forms, do they work as intended?

Exercise 20 - Revision

1. In terms of productivity, divide the following statements into those which represent a benefit of using an IT solution for a task and those which represent a drawback (compared with an alternative non-IT solution).

    a) The task does not require as many staff to operate it

    b) The task requires more people to operate it

    c) The task requires highly skilled people to operate it

    d) The task requires expensive computer equipment

    e) The task can be completed in less time

    f) The task requires only existing computer equipment

2. Which two of the following would be ways of increasing the productivity of your completed task?

    a) Automate more of the functions within the solution

    b) Increase the number of different applications used in the solution

    c) Add shortcuts to save time when running the solution

    d) Add a musical background

Exercise 21 - Summary

Guidelines

The assessment for this unit will be in <u>two</u> parts – **Performance** and **Knowledge**.

In the **Performance** part of the test you will be presented with a scenario describing a real-world problem. It is up to <u>you</u> to choose the most suitable software application for the job (i.e. *Word*, *Excel*, *PowerPoint or Access*), and then make best use of the software to create an IT solution to the problem.

All required content, text, numbers, and images will be provided, but you will need to do some form of editing and formatting. The application you choose to do this should reflect the most appropriate and productive use of IT, and you must demonstrate good, professional practice when developing your solution. Remember – not everyone who may access the data will have the same skills as you.

In the **Knowledge** part of the test, you will be given 12 multi-choice questions relating to the work carried out in the **Performance** part. You will be expected to justify your selection and use of IT for the task, and explain why your chosen software is the most suitable and most productive. You will also need to show that you have considered any relevant legal issues.

This guide has been designed to reinforce the skills needed to choose the most appropriate and productive software for a task, and then to justify that choice and discuss its strengths and weaknesses.

*You will need to be competent in the use of your chosen application(s) to complete the **Performance** part of the test (to a <u>level 3</u> standard). Training in the use of specific software is outside the scope of this guide, however, and is provided in accompanying CiA Training titles.*

Answers

Exercise 8

Step 1   **c)** Only spreadsheet skills are necessary. The required data analysis can be done entirely within *Excel*.

Step 2   **a)** and **b)** An *Excel* application is required to create the scenarios and a printer will be required to print out the report.

Step 3   **c)** The scenarios feature allows you to change/manipulate the data whenever required and perform analysis easily.

Step 4   **c)** If you are using images that are not your property, Copyright law is of primary importance.

Exercise 11

Step 1   **b)** and **c)** These are more likely to have the same framework each time they are run.

Step 2   **b)** This is would replace a number of identical steps. A macro could be written for **a)** but it would be no easier than clicking the **Bold** button. The steps in **c)** are likely to be different every time.

Step 3   **c)**

Step 4   **a)**, **b)** and **c)**. Styles are useful for each of the suggested reasons.

Exercise 16

Step 1   **c)** This refers to the choice of solution.

Step 2   **a)** would represent a strength.

Step 3   **b)** and **c)** Both of these would improve the solution.

Exercise 20

Step 1   Benefits **a)**, **e)**, **f)**.

Drawbacks **b)**, **c)**, **d)**

Step 2   **a)** and **c)** would be the most likely to improve the productivity of the solution.

Glossary

Animation	In presentations, a motion effect which affects objects on a slide or the transition between slides.
Application	A software program such as *Word*.
Clip Art	A range of images available within *Microsoft Office* applications which can be inserted into documents, etc.
Commands	Selections from the **Menu Bar** which perform actions.
Download	Transfer an object from a web site to the user's computer.
Firewall	A filter to control traffic from your PC to the Internet and vice versa.
Font	A type or style of print.
Formatting	Change the way a document, etc. looks.
House Style	A standard set of layout and formatting rules that are applied to all documents, etc. within an organisation.
Linking	Creating a pointer to another item rather than including a copy of it.
Logo	Small, simple graphic that is used to represent an organisation.
Macro	Set of commands that can be run.
Mail Merge	Combining a standard *Word* document with a data source to produce individualised documents (i.e. letters or labels).
Print Preview	A feature that shows how a document will look before it is printed.
Resources	Anything that is a requirement for task, such as people, equipment, software.
Ribbon	The equivalent of the toolbars in *Office 2007* and later.
Template	A framework or base document, etc. that contains certain elements and can be used over and over again to produce consistent output.
Virus	Malicious piece of program designed to enter your system unnoticed.
WordArt	A feature in *Microsoft Word* which allows text to be added as an image.

Index

Other Products from CiA Training

CiA Training is a leading publishing company which has consistently delivered the highest quality products since 1985. Our experienced in-house publishing team has developed a wide range of flexible and easy to use self-teach resources for individual learners and corporate clients all over the world.

At the time of publication, we currently offer approved ECDL materials for:

- **ECDL Syllabus 5.0**

- **ECDL Syllabus 5.0 Revision Series**

- **ECDL Advanced Syllabus 2.0**

- **ECDL Advanced Syllabus 2.0 Revision Series**

Previous syllabus versions are also available upon request.

We hope you have enjoyed using this guide and would love to hear your opinions about our materials. To let us know how we're doing, and to get up to the minute information on our current range of products, please visit us at:

www.ciatraining.co.uk